HADES

By Christine Ha

APEX

WWW.APEXEDITIONS.COM

Apex is distributed by North Star Editions:
sales@northstareditions.com | 888-417-0195

Produced for Apex by Red Line Editorial.

Photographs ©: Prisma/Newscom, cover, 1; Shutterstock Images, 4–5, 6–7, 8–9, 12, 13, 18–19, 20–21, 22–23, 24–25, 26–27, 29; iStockphoto, 10–11, 14–15, 16–17, 20; Lanmas/Alamy, 27

Library of Congress Control Number: 2020952909

ISBN
978-1-63738-014-7 (hardcover)
978-1-63738-050-5 (paperback)
978-1-63738-120-5 (ebook pdf)
978-1-63738-086-4 (hosted ebook)

Printed in the United States of America
Mankato, MN
082021

NOTE TO PARENTS AND EDUCATORS

Apex books are designed to build literacy skills in striving readers. Exciting, high-interest content attracts and holds readers' attention. The text is carefully leveled to allow students to achieve success quickly. Additional features, such as bolded glossary words for difficult terms, help build comprehension.

TABLE OF CONTENTS

CHAPTER 1

A LONG WALK

The **underworld** was dark and quiet. Suddenly, Hades heard music. A man was singing about his wife. He begged Hades to let her come back to life.

Hades ruled the underworld. Myths said people went to this dark place after they died.

Hades agreed. The wife could leave the underworld. But the lovers had to walk single file. And they could not look back.

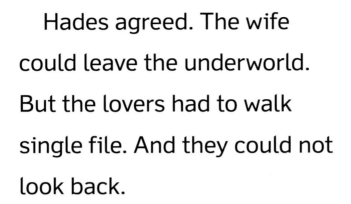

The man's name was Orpheus. He was a talented musician. He sang and played the lyre.

Orpheus used music to sneak into the underworld and get Hades to help.

The god Hermes (left) led people to the underworld after they died.

The lovers almost made it. But near the end, the man turned around. As soon as he did, his wife vanished. Hades wouldn't give them another chance.

THREE KINGS

Hades and his brothers ruled the three parts of the world. Hades was king of the underworld. Poseidon controlled the oceans. Zeus ruled the skies.

CHAPTER 2

LAND OF THE DEAD

Hades was the ruler of the dead. He lived in the underworld. The Greeks believed people's souls went there after they died.

In some myths, the underworld is deep underground. In others, it's beyond the sea.

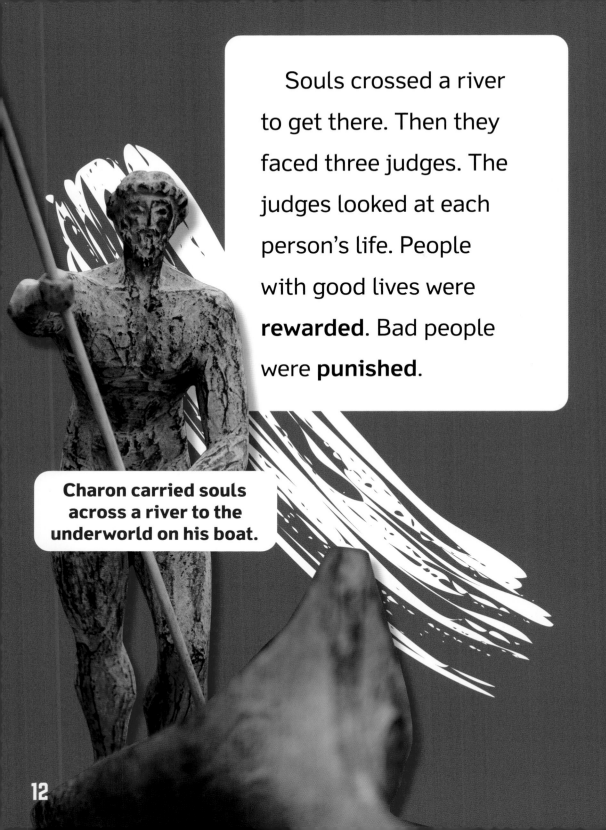

Souls crossed a river to get there. Then they faced three judges. The judges looked at each person's life. People with good lives were **rewarded**. Bad people were **punished**.

Charon carried souls across a river to the underworld on his boat.

Greek coins often had pictures of gods or famous leaders.

A FINAL FEE

Souls had to pay to cross the river to the underworld. Otherwise, they got stuck on its shores for 100 years. So, the Greeks buried people with coins in their mouths.

The three-headed dog's name was Cerberus.

A three-headed dog helped Hades guard the underworld. It made sure no one escaped.

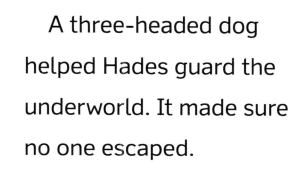

Hades often wore a helmet. It made him invisible.

HADES AND PERSEPHONE

Hades was **stern** and serious. But in one story, he fell in love with Persephone. He brought her to his palace in the underworld.

Hades took Persephone away from her mother, the goddess Demeter.

Persephone's mother was heartbroken. She created a **drought**. Many people died.

Persephone was the daughter of Zeus and Demeter.

Demeter was the goddess of agriculture. She had power over plants and farming.

According to myths, anyone who ate food in the underworld had to stay there.

Hades got Persephone to eat part of a pomegranate, so she had to stay in the underworld.

20

Finally, Hades let Persephone return to Earth. But she could only stay for part of the year. For the other part, she would live with Hades.

Plants grew when Persephone left the underworld.

CHANGING SEASONS

The myth of Persephone explained the seasons. Winter happened when she was in the underworld. Spring came when she returned. Flowers blossomed. Plants grew.

CHAPTER 4

HONORING HADES

Hades had few temples. And he was not often shown in art. However, he was greatly **respected**.

The Greeks believed some temples of Hades held doors to the underworld.

In art, Hades is often shown with Persephone and Cerberus.

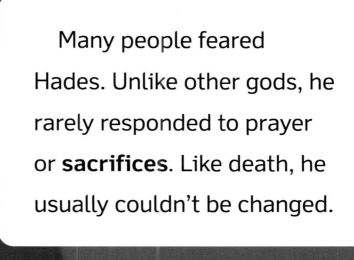

Many people feared Hades. Unlike other gods, he rarely responded to prayer or **sacrifices**. Like death, he usually couldn't be changed.

HADES IN ART

When he is shown in art, Hades usually holds one of two things. The first is a key to the underworld. The second is a spear. It has two sharp points.

Some Greeks refused to say his name out loud. They feared it would cause death. Instead, they used other names to **refer** to Hades. One was Plouton. This name means "wealthy."

A place dedicated to Hades was sometimes called a ploutonion.

The Romans had their own versions of the Greek gods. In Rome, Hades was known as Pluto.

The name Hades means "the unseen one."

COMPREHENSION QUESTIONS

Write your answers on a separate piece of paper.

1. Write a couple sentences describing the main ideas of Chapter 4.

2. Do you think it was fair for Hades to punish both lovers when the man looked back? Why or why not?

3. Who did Hades fall in love with?
   - **A.** Demeter
   - **B.** Persephone
   - **C.** Eurydice

4. Why didn't Hades appear in much Greek art?
   - **A.** The Greeks did not believe in Hades.
   - **B.** The Greeks did not respect Hades.
   - **C.** The Greeks were afraid of Hades.

5. What does **musician** mean in this book?

*He was a talented **musician**. He sang and played the lyre.*

    A. a person who makes food

    B. a person who makes music

    C. a person who dislikes music

6. What does **blossomed** mean in this book?

*Spring came when she returned. Flowers **blossomed**. Plants grew.*

    A. had open petals

    B. shrank and died

    C. became very cold

Answer key on page 32.

GLOSSARY

drought
A time of little or no rain.

invisible
Not able to be seen.

lyre
A stringed instrument that is similar to a small harp.

punished
Forced to do something hard or painful after doing something wrong.

refer
To talk about someone or something.

respected
Admired or seen as important.

rewarded
Given gifts or honors for doing good things.

sacrifices
Gifts to gods or goddesses to win their help or favor.

stern
Serious and firm, especially in making people follow the rules.

underworld
The land of the dead.

TO LEARN MORE

BOOKS

Bell, Samantha S. *Ancient Greece.* Lake Elmo, MN: Focus Readers, 2020.

Menzies, Jean. *Greek Myths: Meet the Heroes, Gods, and Monsters of Ancient Greece.* New York: DK Publishing, 2020.

Temple, Teri. *Hades: God of the Underworld.* Mankato, MN: The Child's World, 2019.

ONLINE RESOURCES

Visit **www.apexeditions.com** to find links and resources related to this title.

ABOUT THE AUTHOR

Christine Ha lives in Minnesota. She enjoys reading and learning about myths and legends from around the world.

INDEX

Answer Key:
1. Answers will vary; **2.** Answers will vary; **3.** B; **4.** C; **5.** B; **6.** A